Questions and Answers
SCIENCE • NATURE

Author: Louise Spilsbury

Consultants: Tony Sizer, John Williams, David Lambert, Simon Adams,
Mandy Holloway, Steve Parker

Original edition produced by Tall Tree Ltd, London

This edition published by Parragon in 2008

Parragon
Queen Street House
4 Queen Street
Bath BA1 1HE, UK

ISBN 978-1-4075-1898-5

Printed in Indonesia

Questions and Answers
SCIENCE • NATURE

The **What**, **When**, **Where**, **How** and **Why**
of everything you need to know about science and nature

PaRragon

Bath · New York · Singapore · Hong Kong · Cologne · Delhi · Melbourne

CONTENTS

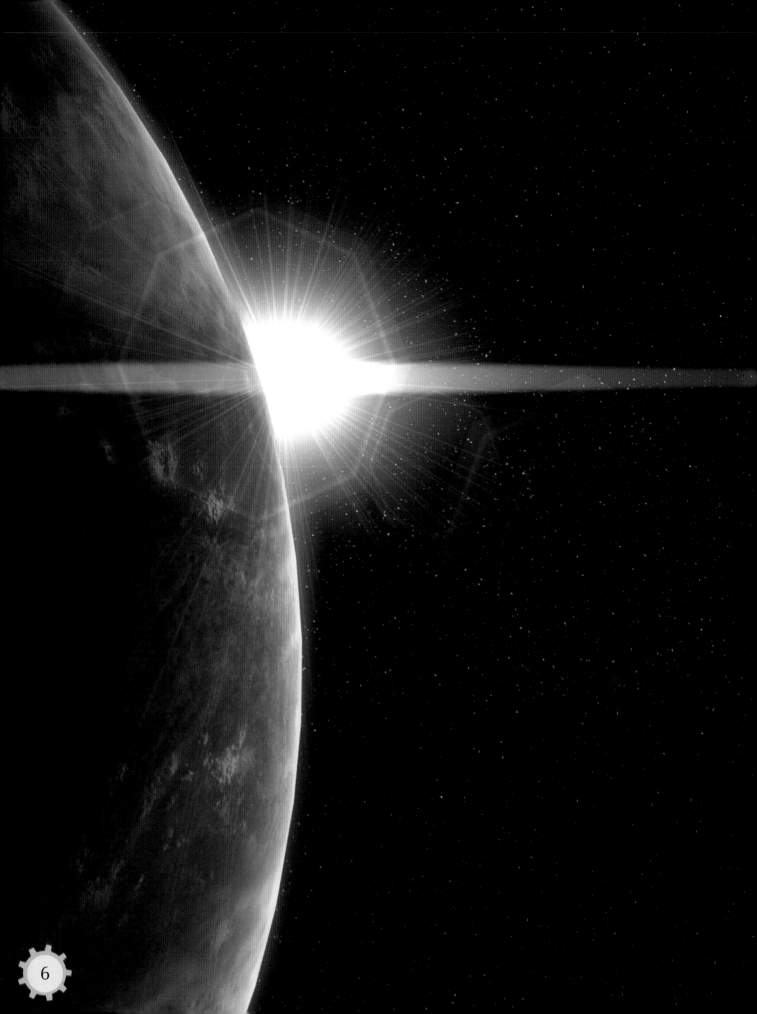

EARTH AND SPACE

The Earth is one of a group of planets that orbit the enormous ball of burning gas that is the Sun. Although you might think that the Earth is huge, it is only a tiny speck when compared with the vast size of the Universe with its billions of stars and galaxies. On its surface, the Earth is a restless, changing planet, with erupting volcanoes, shaking earthquakes and powerful forces that are continuously changing the landscape.

THE BIG BANG

What was the Big Bang?

The Big Bang was an explosion that created the whole Universe. About 14 billion years ago, the Universe exploded outwards from a hot, dense bubble that was smaller than a pinhead. The Universe quickly grew larger than a galaxy and kept on expanding. As it slowly cooled, tiny particles (pieces) within it joined and began to form the stars and planets.

The Big Bang exploded from a tiny point, called a singularity.

BELOW Stars begin as clouds of gas like this, called nebulae.

When did the first stars shine?

The first stars began to shine about 300 million years after the Big Bang. Particles began to clump together and formed clouds of gas. These slowly grew and became hotter and hotter. Eventually, the centre of these clouds became so hot that the clouds exploded and became the balls of fire we call stars. New stars are born and die every day.

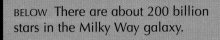
BELOW There are about 200 billion stars in the Milky Way galaxy.

HOW many galaxies are there?

There are more than 100 billion galaxies in the Universe. A galaxy is a large group of stars, dust, gas, rocks and planets. Most stars in the Universe are found in galaxies. The Sun and planet Earth are part of our galaxy, the Milky Way. Astronomers have photographed many galaxies through special telescopes. With the naked eye, people can only see three galaxies beyond the Milky Way.

DID YOU KNOW?
Some of the stars we can see in the night sky are so far away that the light coming from them has taken millions of years to reach Earth.

A telescope uses glass lenses to magnify distant objects.

Is the Universe changing?

Yes, the Universe is still growing and expanding today. Some scientists believe that the Universe will keep expanding. Others think that the expansion will start to slow and eventually stop. They believe that the Universe will then start to shrink until it crunches together into a tiny space and sparks off another Big Bang.

9

THE SUN

What is the Sun?

The Sun is just an ordinary star, one of billions of stars in the Universe. The Sun has a special name and is important to us because it is close enough to give Earth light and warmth. This light and warmth is what allows plants, animals and other living things to survive on our planet. Without the Sun there would be no life on Earth.

Close-up pictures of the Sun show the hot gases gushing out from its surface.

BELOW Solar panels like these trap some of the Sun's energy and change it into electricity we can use. The word solar means 'to do with the Sun'.

How hot is the Sun?

The temperature at the core, or centre, of the Sun is about 16 million Celsius. From the core, this incredible heat energy flows to the surface, where the temperature is closer to 6,000 Celsius. This is still so incredibly hot that it would melt anything it touched.

Why is the Sun so bright?

The Sun is the brightest object in the sky because it is a giant ball of brightly glowing gas. Light from the Sun takes just over eight minutes to reach Earth, but when it gets here it is still so powerful that the light can damage your eyesight. That is why you should never look at the Sun directly and always wear sunglasses on sunny days.

DID YOU KNOW?
The Sun is about five billion years old and it is more than one million kilometres wide. It is so big that more than one million Earths could fit inside it.

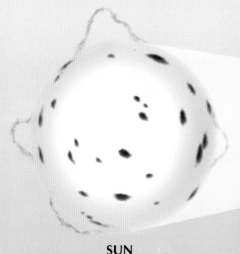

solar eclipse seen here

MOON

EARTH

SUN

ABOVE The Sun is about 400 times wider than the Moon. However, because the Moon is about 400 times closer to Earth than the Sun, they both look about the same size in the sky from Earth.

When do solar eclipses happen?

The Moon travels around Earth. A solar eclipse happens when the Moon comes in between the Sun and the Earth and casts a huge shadow onto the Earth. A total eclipse is rare, but when it happens, the Sun seems to disappear from the sky and for a few moments everything becomes cold and dark.

THE SOLAR SYSTEM

SUN

MERCURY

VENUS

EARTH

MARS

JUPITER

SATURN
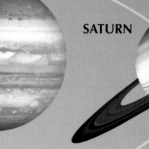

What is the solar system?

The solar system consists of the Sun and the planets that move around the Sun in oval paths called orbits. A planet is a vast ball of rock or gas that travels in orbit around a star. There are other objects in our solar system, too, such as moons and asteroids.

DID YOU KNOW?
The Sun is so far away that if you tried to drive there, travelling at 100 kilometres an hour, it would take you 170 years to reach your destination!

How far are we from the Sun?

Earth is 150 million kilometres away from the Sun. This means that our planet is far enough away from the Sun for water to be liquid. If Earth were closer and, therefore, warmer, water would turn to gas, and if it were farther away, water would become ice. It is Earth's distance from the Sun that makes it the only planet in the solar system that is known to support life.

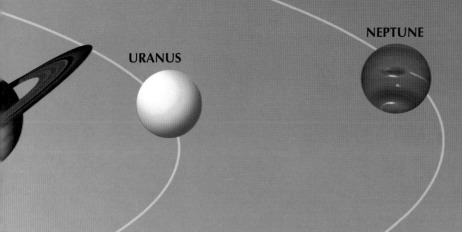

URANUS

NEPTUNE

PLUTO

These are the nine planets of our solar system. Earth is the third planet from the Sun.

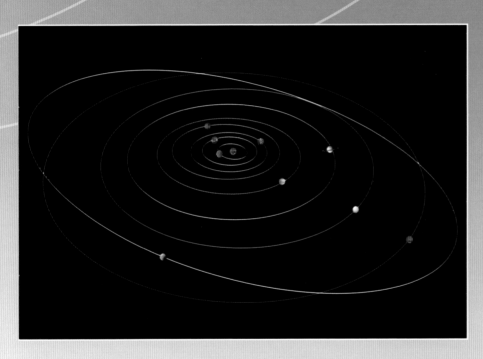

Why do planets orbit the Sun?

The planets move around the Sun because the Sun is so big that its gravity is very powerful. Gravity is the force that pulls the planets towards the Sun. It is strong enough to hold all the planets in the solar system in their orbits, moving around the Sun in the same direction.

When did Earth form?

Earth and the other planets formed about five billion years ago. Our planet was born from dust and gases whirling in orbit around the Sun as it was forming. In the intense heat, the dust and gases collided and hardened into a ball of rock. Even today, Earth is still hit by dust from space and the occasional large piece of rock.

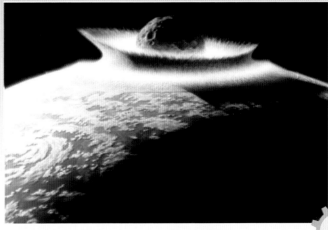

THE ROCKY PLANETS

Which are the rocky planets?

Mercury, Venus, Earth and Mars are known as the rocky planets because they are mainly made of rock and metal. Mercury is closest to the Sun. Although it is burning hot on this planet during the day, at night it becomes freezing cold. This is because Mercury's atmosphere is very thin and there are no clouds to trap and hold warmth during the night.

We cannot see the surface of Venus because it is always covered in thick clouds.

MERCURY

VENUS

Where is the hottest planet?

Although Venus is the second planet from the Sun, it has the hottest surface. It is hotter than Mercury because it has a blanket of fast-moving clouds around it. This traps heat from the Sun and stops the heat flowing out into space. The thick atmosphere on Venus is mostly made up of carbon dioxide gas, which would be deadly poisonous for people.

Why is Earth called the blue planet?

Earth is often called the blue planet, because three quarters of its surface is covered in water and from space it looks blue. When Earth formed, a layer of gas formed around it. This layer protects the Earth from getting too hot or too cold. Eventually, rain began to fall and formed our planet's rivers, lakes and oceans.

DID YOU KNOW?
Some scientists believe there could be life on Mars. Although it is too cold for life to exist on the surface, tiny organisms could exist in warmer pockets below the ground.

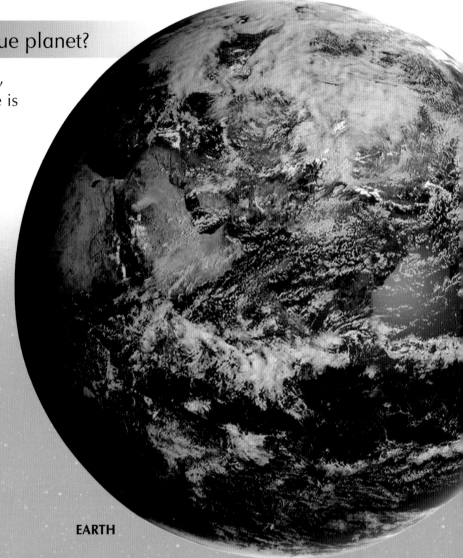

EARTH

MARS

What makes Mars red?

Mars is known as the red planet because of the colour of its soil. The surface of Mars is rich in iron oxide, which is rust and has a reddish colour. Mars has little atmosphere and gets very cold. Like Earth, it has ice caps on its north pole and south pole but the rest of its surface is a dusty red desert.

THE GAS PLANETS

What are the gas planets?

Jupiter, Saturn, Uranus and Neptune are known as the gas planets. These planets are large spinning balls of gas with small rocky cores (centres). Jupiter and Saturn are also known as the giant planets because they are so big. Jupiter is twice as heavy as all the other planets put together and Saturn is almost as large as Jupiter.

Jupiter is the largest planet in the solar system. The bright colours you can see are formed by the different gases in Jupiter's clouds.

BELOW Saturn's famous rings orbit around its middle. The rings are very thin compared to the size of the planet, none being more than 50 metres deep.

Why does Saturn have rings?

Saturn's rings are made up of dust and pieces of rock and ice. Astronomers think that the dust and rock may have come from moons that broke up when they crashed into other objects in space. The millions of chunks of ice-covered rock that form the colourful rings are held in orbit around Saturn by the pull of the planet's gravity.

How many moons does Jupiter have?

Jupiter has 63 moons, and possibly more. A moon is an object that orbits around a planet. Some moons are rocky and round, but they can be icy or volcanic. Jupiter also has rings, like Saturn, but they are smaller and fainter. Uranus and Neptune have rings, too.

ABOVE If you look at Jupiter with binoculars, you can easily see its four main moons. Italian astronomer Galileo Galilei was the first person to spot these moons, along with Saturn's rings, in 1610, using an early telescope.

DID YOU KNOW?
Some of the billions of bits of dust, rock and ice that make up Saturn's rings are as big as a house. Others are as small as grains of sand.

When were Uranus, Neptune and Pluto discovered?

Astronomers discovered Uranus, Neptune and Pluto later than the other planets because these planets are so far away. Uranus was spotted in 1781, Neptune in 1846 and Pluto, which is five times smaller than Earth, in 1930. Pluto is so small some astronomers argue that it is not a planet at all. It is also so far away that no maps have yet been made of its surface.

URANUS

PLUTO

NEPTUNE

THE MOON

How big is the Moon?

The Moon is about a quarter of the size of Earth and measures 3,476 kilometres wide. The Moon is Earth's only natural satellite and is held in orbit by the pull of Earth's gravity. It takes the Moon about four weeks to complete one orbit of the Earth. Our word 'month', which means a period of about four weeks, comes from the word 'Moon'.

DID YOU KNOW?
There is no such thing as moonlight. Moonlight is simply the Sun's light reflected off the Moon's surface. The Moon itself gives off no light.

BELOW Scientists believe that there are large amounts of frozen water hidden in craters on the Moon's surface. A crater appears as a dark shadow on the Moon's surface.

crater

sea

Why is the Moon covered in craters?

The Moon's atmosphere is very thin and gives no protection against rocks from space that smash into the surface. These impacts create large dips called craters. Some craters are huge and were made by rocks as big as mountains. Most of the Moon's surface is covered in dust. There are also parts called 'seas' that are not water but dried lava that poured from volcanoes long ago.

Crescent Moon · Full Moon · Crescent Moon

What are the Moon's phases?

The different shapes the Moon appears to take throughout the month are called the phases of the Moon. When we see the whole Moon, we call it a full Moon. When we cannot see the Moon at all, we call it a new Moon. When we can see only a thin sliver of the Moon, we call it a crescent Moon. The Moon doesn't change shape – we just see different parts of it when it is in different stages of its orbit around Earth.

ABOVE These are the Moon's phases as we see them throughout the month. The Moon's shape changes from a thin crescent to a circle and back again.

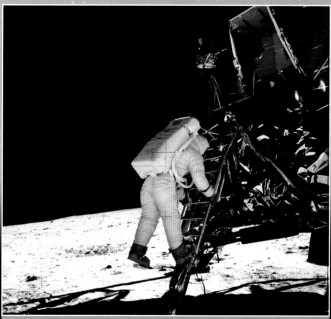

Who was the first person on the Moon?

American astronaut Neil Armstrong was the first person on the Moon. As he left his landing craft on 21 July 1969, he said, 'That's one small step for man but one giant leap for mankind.' He and fellow astronaut Edwin 'Buzz' Aldrin collected soil samples and took photos. The Moon's weak gravity meant it was easy to move around, but they had to wear spacesuits because there is no air there and the Sun's light is very harsh.

OUR EARTH

mantle

Why do we have seasons?

The Earth has seasons because it is tilted at an angle. This means that as it orbits around the Sun different parts are tilted towards the Sun. When the northern hemisphere, or top half of the Earth, points to the Sun, this area gets summer. At the same time, the southern hemisphere, or bottom half of the Earth, is pointing away from the Sun and this area experiences its winter.

LEFT Seen here is the same meadow in summer (top), autumn (middle) and winter (bottom).

What causes night and day?

Night and day happen because the Earth rotates, or makes one complete turn, every 24 hours. As well as travelling in an orbit around the Sun, planet Earth spins around its axis, an imaginary line going through the North and South Poles. This means that at any one time, half of the Earth is facing the Sun and has daytime, while the other half faces away from the Sun, so it has night.

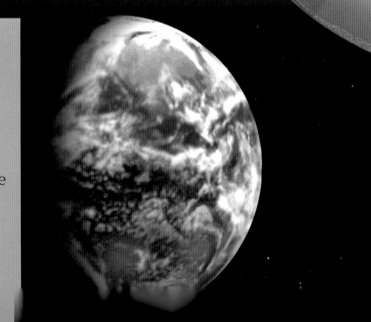

outer core

What is inside the Earth?

Inside the centre of the Earth there is red-hot, liquid rock. This rock is called magma. The land and oceans at the Earth's surface lie on an outer layer of cool, hard rock called the crust. The hot magma below rises and sinks slowly in a layer called the mantle. At the very centre of the Earth is a super-hot ball of iron called the core.

DID YOU KNOW?
The Earth's surface is cracked into large pieces, called plates, which fit together like an enormous jigsaw. There are nine large plates and several smaller ones.

crust

core

60 million years ago

155 million years ago

How did the land divide into continents?

The land sits on top of the large pieces, or plates, that make up the Earth's surface. These plates are slowly moving. Before about 200 million years ago, all the land was joined to form one big continent, or super continent. Over millions of years, as the plates moved, the land split and slowly divided into the seven continents we know today: Africa, Antarctica, Asia, Australia, Europe, North America and South America.

200 million years ago

VOLCANOES AND EARTHQUAKES

Why do volcanoes erupt?

Volcanoes erupt when some of the hot magma (liquid rock) from below the Earth's surface squeezes up through holes in the surface. Magma is so hot that it melts solid rock in its path and makes a tunnel through the crust just below the surface. Gradually, more and more magma builds up there, until suddenly the volcano erupts and the hot liquid rock spurts into the air.

What is a volcanic island?

When a volcano erupts on the ocean floor, the hot liquid rock cools and sets into hard rock. Each time the volcano erupts, it gets a bit larger as more liquid rock piles up and hardens on its sides. Eventually, it becomes a tall underwater mountain with its tip sticking out above the water, forming an island.

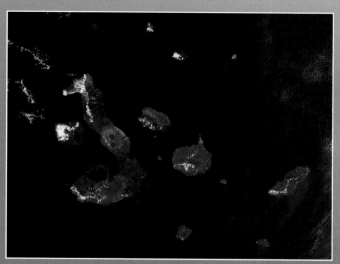

LEFT A string of islands can form when a plate in the Earth's crust glides slowly over a hole in the mantle where magma is released. The Galapagos Islands formed in this way.

RIGHT Most earthquakes last for less than a minute, but their force can be felt over a huge area.

DID YOU KNOW?

Several million earthquakes happen around the world every year, but most are so small that people do not even know they have happened.

BELOW Tsunamis are giant waves caused by earthquakes under water. They can cause great damage when they hit the shore, leaving behind wrecked homes.

Why do earthquakes happen?

Earthquakes happen because the plates that make up the Earth's crust are moving like giant rafts on the bubbling magma below. These plates usually slide against each other gently, but sometimes two plates get stuck and push hard against each other. When they suddenly jolt apart again, this sudden movement creates the violent shaking at the Earth's surface known as earthquakes.

How do earthquakes cause damage?

When small earthquakes shake the land they may simply knock books from shelves, but large earthquakes can make buildings and roads crumble. They can create huge cracks in the land into which whole lakes disappear. Some earthquakes set off landslides, where huge amounts of soil slide down a hill and bury buildings at the bottom.

MOUNTAINS AND VALLEYS

How do mountains form?

Some mountains form from volcanoes. Dome mountains occur where magma near the Earth's surface forms a rounded bulge of rock, but does not erupt to become a volcano. Fold mountains form when two colliding plates cause the Earth's crust to buckle and fold, making mountain ranges. Block mountains form when fractures in the Earth's crust push a block of rock upwards.

Do mountains continue to grow?

Yes, some mountains continue to get taller after they first form! For example, the Himalayas are growing by about 6 centimetres every year. The Himalayas were formed 50 million years ago when two of the Earth's plates collided. As the plates continue to push into each other the mountains are gradually getting higher and even harder to climb!

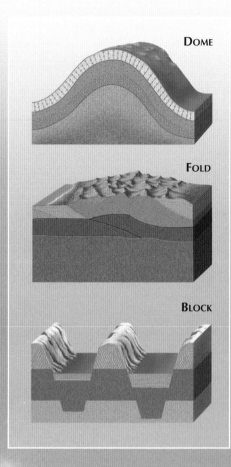

DOME

FOLD

BLOCK

DID YOU KNOW?
The Mid-Atlantic Ocean Ridge is an underwater mountain range. It is as long as the Rocky, Andes and Himalaya mountain ranges combined.

What is a glacier?

A glacier is a huge river of ice. A build-up of snow and ice in very cold, high mountain areas causes the river of ice to flow downhill. Most glaciers flow so slowly you cannot tell they are moving. As glaciers move, they carry rocks along with them that help gouge out deep grooves, or valleys, into the land through which they pass.

Mountain glaciers have created many of the valleys on the Earth's surface.

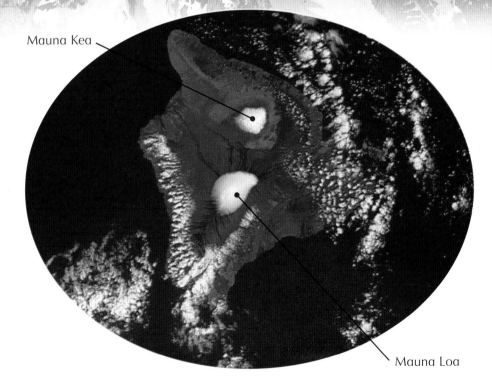

Mauna Kea

Mauna Loa

Where is the tallest mountain?

The tallest mountain is Mauna Kea on Hawaii Island. It measures 10,203 metres from base to peak, but most of it is underwater. Only 4,205 metres of it are above sea level. On land, Mount Everest is the highest mountain, reaching 8,850 metres above sea level. Also on Hawaii Island is Mauna Loa, the world's biggest volcano.

WEATHER AND CLIMATE

What is climate?

A region's climate is the type of weather it gets throughout the year. Scientists split the world into five major climate zones. Tropical areas have hot, wet climates. Areas with dry climates get little rain. Temperate areas have cool winters and warm summers. Continental climates have cold winters and mild summers. Polar climates have freezing temperatures all year round.

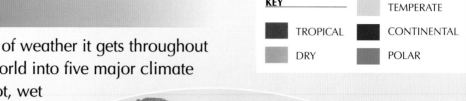

KEY

	TEMPERATE
TROPICAL	CONTINENTAL
DRY	POLAR

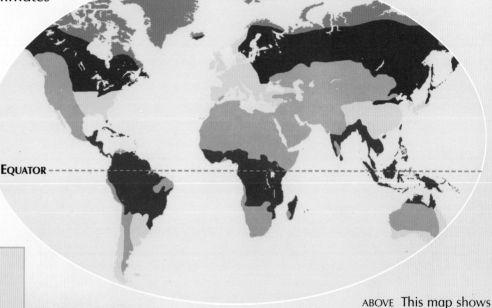

EQUATOR -

ABOVE This map shows where the world's five main climate zones are found.

DID YOU KNOW?
In freezing conditions, water falling from the sky becomes snow or hail. Hailstones are balls of ice. Some can be the size of a large grapefruit!

Why do winds blow?

Wind is moving air, and winds blow when air temperatures change. When the Sun shines, it heats a patch of air. Warm air is lighter than cold air, so the warm air rises. Cooler air moves into the spaces the warm air left behind. These air movements are what we know as wind. When air moves quickly it can be a howling gale. Small air movements can create a gentle breeze.

When does it rain?

Raindrops are part of the water cycle – the continuous movement of water between Earth and sky. When the Sun heats water at the surface of oceans and lakes some of it turns into water vapour, a gas in the air. When water vapour rises high in the air, where it is cold, it cools and turns back into water droplets. These gather in clouds and then fall back to Earth as rain. The cycle then begins again.

Water vapour collects to form clouds.

Water falls as rain.

Water turns into water vapour.

Water flows into seas.

Water flows downhill in streams and rivers.

How do people forecast the weather?

Meteorologists are scientists who study the weather. They have many ways of predicting the weather. They use balloons that float in the air to record temperature and humidity (the amount of water in the air). They use photographs of the Earth taken from space so they can see the direction in which storms are blowing. Weather stations around the world share data through computers in order to keep people informed about the weather.

DINOSAURS AND PREHISTORIC LIFE

Three hundred million years before humans first stood upright, reptiles known as dinosaurs ruled supreme. Some evolved to become the largest land animals ever to walk the Earth. Others were savage predators. The dinosaurs' reign ended about 65 million years ago, probably when a asteroid smashed into the Earth and caused them to become extinct. In the periods that followed, mammals were the dominant species, evolving to produce some amazing creatures, including, eventually, us.

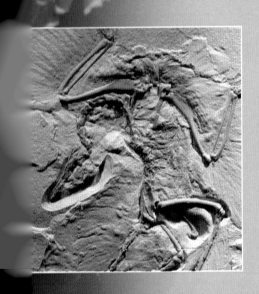

RECORD IN THE ROCKS

What is a fossil?

A fossil is the remains of a plant or animal that lived millions of years ago. Fossils are a record of what lived on Earth in prehistoric times, the period before humans existed or began to write about the world. Without fossils, we would not know about ancient living things, such as dinosaurs.

ABOVE Some fossils are insects that were trapped in tree sap. The sap hardened to form amber like this.

DID YOU KNOW?
People have found fossils of sea creatures at the tops of mountains. This is because, over millions of years, the seabed was lifted up and formed mountains. Weather wore the rock away, exposing the fossils.

How do fossils form?

Fossils form in different ways. Some fossils form when an animal, such as a shellfish, dies. It sinks to the bottom of the sea and is slowly covered in muddy sediment. Over millions of years, the sediment hardens into rock. Meanwhile, the animal's body rots away and is replaced by mineral substances. As these harden they form rock shaped like the animal. This is called a fossil cast.

Millions of years ago, a sea creature called an ammonite dies.

It sinks to the bottom of the sea and is covered in sediment.

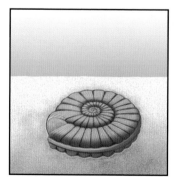

The ammonite rots away and minerals replace it.

The minerals harden into rock and form a fossil.

When do the oldest fossils date from?

The oldest fossils that have been found are from around 3,500 million years ago. These fossils are also the smallest ever found. They are the remains of bacteria, tiny living things that formed a kind of slime in ancient pools and seas. The oldest fossils with hard parts, such as shells, are about 545 million years old.

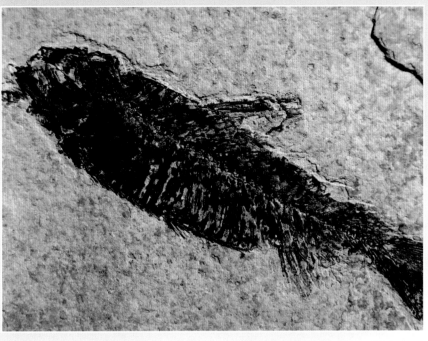

ABOVE Many fossils are of fish and other sea creatures because most fossils formed in the sea.

BELOW These fossil footsteps were left by a prehistoric creature millions of years ago.

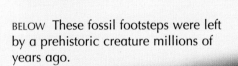

What do fossils tell us?

Fossils tell us lots about the plants and animals that lived long ago. For example, by piecing together fossil dinosaur bones, scientists have learned how dinosaurs moved and hunted. Using fossils, they can tell when some animals died out and when new kinds of animals first appeared. Fossils help scientists understand how life on Earth grew from a few tiny living things to the great variety we know today.

THE BEGINNING OF LIFE

When did life on Earth begin?

Life on Earth began about 3,500 million years ago. When Earth first formed, it was too hot for life to exist. The first living things were bacteria, which developed in deep-sea springs or muddy pools near volcanoes (right), after the Earth had cooled. The bacteria took their energy from chemicals in water, and slowly developed into more complex life forms, a process known as evolution.

ABOVE Stromatolites are layers of blue-green algae and rock. These algae were among the earliest living things to make food by photosynthesis.

How did living things develop?

Many new living things began to develop by 3,000 million years ago, after some early life forms found a way of getting energy from sunlight and using it to make food. This process is called photosynthesis. During photosynthesis, living things release the gas oxygen. Many more living things then developed to breathe the new oxygen in the atmosphere.

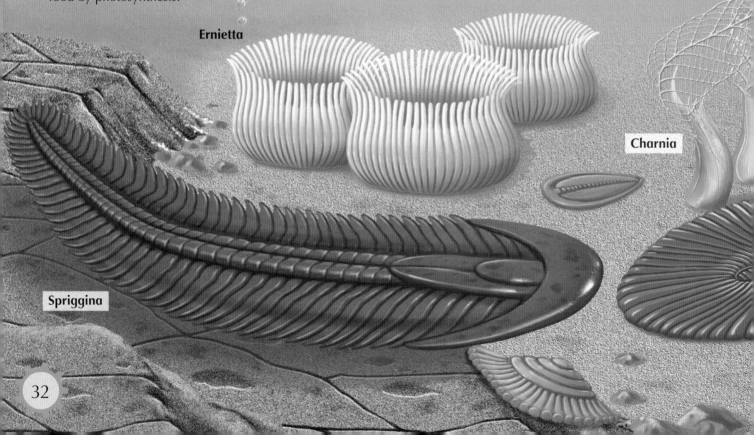

Ernietta

Charnia

Spriggina

What were the first animals like?

The first animals probably looked a little like tiny tadpoles. They lived in the shallow seas that covered Earth about 1,200 million years ago and thrived on the new supplies of oxygen in the atmosphere. Slowly, these tiny animals grew together in clusters and developed into the first sponges.

DID YOU KNOW?
Some of the kinds of animals that first lived long ago still exist today, such as the starfishes. However, most are extinct, which means they all died out.

Where did early animals live?

Early animals, such as sponges, jellyfish and sea pens, all lived on the sea floor. They fed on bits of dead plants and animals in the mud or water. At this stage, there was no need for them to move because there were no predators (hunters).

Pteridinium

Jelly blobs

Cyclomedusa

Parvancorina

Tribrachidium

Dickinsonia

ABOVE Early animals lived on the sea floor and had no need to move.

33

GIANT FORESTS AND INSECTS

ABOVE A fossilized fern

When did plants first grow on land?

Plants first began to grow on land around 475 million years ago. These plants lived in swamps and on the muddy shores of rivers. They probably had a waxy coating to stop the salty water and the sun from drying them out. Plants gradually developed roots to reach water underground. They soon spread beyond the shores and began to turn the land green.

Why did early plants grow so big?

Early plants were able to grow so big because of the climate long ago. In many places, the air was damp and steamy, rather like it is in tropical jungles today. As plants crowded together, they grew taller and taller as they competed for the light. Plants in the great early forests included huge horsetails, club mosses and ferns up to 50 metres tall. That is as high as 10 double-decker buses stacked on top of each other!

DID YOU KNOW?
Over millions of years, the giant trees and plants from the swamps of this time rotted and hardened to form the coal we burn today.

Tree fern

RIGHT This giant swampy forest is from about 300 million years ago. Some plants and insects were much bigger than their relatives alive today.

What were the first insects like?

The first insects were probably the bristletails, which were the size of a large prawn. They had no wings and scurried about the ancient swamps on little legs. They used their bristles to sense movements in the air that warned them a predator was about. They had claws on their mouthparts that they used to feed on plants and waste.

How big were the first dragonflies?

Some of the first dragonflies had a wingspan of up to a metre. They flew over pools, using their large eyes to look for other insects to eat. Winged insects first appeared around 400 million years ago, and could explore more places to live and find different kinds of food. Soon, many more insect species developed, including cockroaches and grasshoppers.

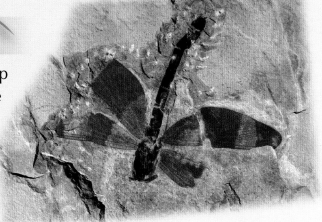

ABOVE A fossilized dragonfly.

Dragonfly

Giant horsetail

Club moss

RISE OF THE REPTILES

What was the first reptile?

The first reptile was probably *Hylonomus*, which lived 315 million years ago. *Hylonomus* was 20 centimetres long and looked rather like a modern lizard. Reptiles like these evolved from a group of amphibian-like tetrapods that laid their eggs on land. Inside the eggs, the young fed on yolks, which made them strong and more likely to survive. Reptiles soon became the dominant animals on land.

RIGHT *Hylonomus* used its small sharp teeth to eat millipedes and early insects.

Which reptiles had armoured bodies?

BELOW This early turtle had a heavily armoured shell.

The group of reptiles known as pareiasaurs had plates of bony armour over their bodies. They lived about 260 million years ago. One type of pareiasaur was *Scutosaurus*, which means 'shield lizard'. Although it grew to about 3 metres long and was large and powerful, it was a plant eater. Some of the first tortoises and turtles, which evolved about 50 million years later, were as big as *Scutosaurus*.

Why did *Dimetrodon* have a sail on its back?

Scientists do not know for sure why *Dimetrodon* had a spiny sail on its back. Perhaps this reptile-like creature used the sail to soak up warmth from the sun when it was cold or to give off heat to cool down on hot days. Other theories are that it could have been used to attract mates or to scare off other animals.

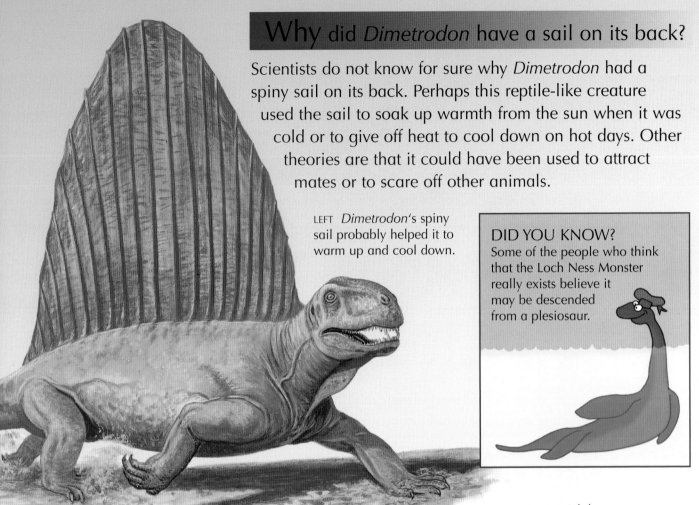

LEFT *Dimetrodon*'s spiny sail probably helped it to warm up and cool down.

DID YOU KNOW?
Some of the people who think that the Loch Ness Monster really exists believe it may be descended from a plesiosaur.

BELOW Ichthyosaurs were sleek, fast-swimming reptiles.

Did early reptiles ever live in water?

Some early reptiles lived permanently in water. The plesiosaurs had large paddle-like legs for moving through the water and long necks for reaching out to catch fish. Ichthyosaurs looked more like large, toothy dolphins. They were swimming in the oceans at the same time as dinosaurs were living on the land.

DAWN OF THE DINOSAURS

When did dinosaurs develop?

The first dinosaurs developed from other reptiles about 230 million years ago. At this time, the world looked very different. There were no birds or mammals, and, although there were ferns and trees, there were no grasses or flowering plants. Vast areas were desert. Dinosaurs dominated the world for 150 million years.

DID YOU KNOW?
Scientists may never be sure what colour dinosaurs were or even whether some had hair.

Brachiosaurus

Why did dinosaurs get so big?

Scientists are not certain why some dinosaurs got so big. Dinosaurs may have developed into larger, stronger and faster animals in order to compete with each other for food. Sauropods were by far the biggest dinosaurs, with long necks to reach leaves at the tops of tall trees. The carnivores may simply have evolved into larger beasts to be able to catch them.

ABOVE *Brachiosaurus* was one of the largest sauropods – gigantic, slow-moving plant eaters. Sauropods included some of the biggest land animals of all time.

Did any dinosaurs live in water?

No, dinosaurs only lived on land. Some reptiles did live in the sea, including *Plesiosaurus*, which was not related to dinosaurs. This large carnivorous animal had a long neck and sharp teeth to catch fish. Other reptiles, such as the pterosaurs, could fly. They had wings made of skin, similar to those of bats.

LEFT *Plesiosaurus* lived in the sea and could grow up to 12 metres long.

What was the smallest dinosaur?

The smallest dinosaurs were not much bigger than a chicken. *Saltopus*, which lived about 220 million years ago, was about 60 centimetres long and scurried along the ground eating insects. *Compsognathus*, which means 'pretty jaw', lived about 150 million years ago and was only about a metre long.

Compsognathus

DINOSAUR RULE

Which dinosaur waddled?

The giant *Megalosaurus* dinosaur probably waddled like a duck. Its tail would have swung to and fro as it walked along. *Megalosaurus* lived in the Jurassic period, when dinosaurs dominated the Earth. It had vicious claws and saw-edged teeth for cutting into the flesh of its prey.

LEFT *Megalosaurus* had saw-edged teeth for cutting into flesh.

Why did *Stegosaurus* have armoured plates?

The rows of armoured plates along *Stegosaurus*'s back probably helped make the dinosaur look bigger to put off predators. Some scientists think that the plates may have been used to display to other stegosaurs. Another group of dinosaurs, the ankylosaurs, also had armoured plates. They even had hard shells on their eyelids.

RIGHT *Stegosaurus* used its spiked tail for defence and its beaked mouth to bite off plants to eat.

DID YOU KNOW?

Argentinosaurus and many other dinosaurs were huge, but the blue whale is bigger than any of them.

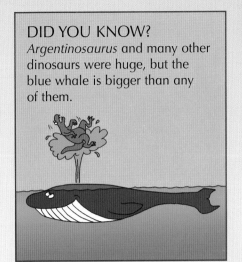

HOW fast could dinosaurs run?

Some dinosaurs, such as *Gallimimus*, may have run up to 60 kilometres an hour. *Gallimimus* was an ostrich-like dinosaur that probably lived in groups. It had a small head with a toothless, beaked mouth and probably ate insects, small animals and eggs. It had long legs and a long tail that helped it to keep its balance when making fast, sharp turns.

Did dinosaurs hunt in packs?

Yes, some dinosaurs might have hunted in packs, working together in order to catch and bring down larger dinosaurs. *Giganotosaurus* was one of the biggest meat-eating dinosaurs ever. It could hunt alone, but to catch a full-grown *Argentinosaurus*, perhaps the largest dinosaur that ever lived, packs of six or more *Giganotosaurus* worked together.

ABOVE *Gallimimus* was up to 6 metres long and about 3.5 metres tall.

BELOW *Argentinosaurus* grew to over 35 metres long. Even so, it was prey to *Giganotosaurus*.

THE LAST DINOSAURS

Which dinosaur had the biggest claws?

Therizinosaurus had the biggest claws. This dinosaur had three curved claws on each of its arms, measuring up to a metre long. It was a herbivore, or plant eater, and it may have used its claws to pull down branches from high trees to eat the bark and leaves.

BELOW *Therizinosaurus* used its enormous claws to reach branches on tall trees.

DID YOU KNOW?
Some of the most common later dinosaurs were the hadrosaurs. They had a toothless beak that looked like that of a duck and are called duck-billed dinosaurs.

RIGHT *Tyrannosaurus rex*'s teeth could be up to 30 centimetres long.

How many teeth did Tyrannosaurus rex have?

Tyrannosaurus rex had over 60 thick, cone-shaped teeth in its metre-long mouth. Some of the teeth were sharp as knives and used to slice off flesh. Others were shaped for crunching bones, so that the animals could eat the bone marrow inside the bones. Although Tyrannosaurus rex is often seen as a fierce and successful hunter, it may also have been a scavenger, eating animals it found that were already dead.

When did *Triceratops* use its horns?

Triceratops probably used its horns to protect itself. When attacked, it probably stood its ground and used them to injure a predator. At about 9 metres long, *Triceratops* was a large plant eater. It may even have been able to take on the mighty *Tyrannosaurus rex*. Scientists think that the bony frill around their necks enabled the different *Triceratops* in a herd to tell each other apart.

Why did dinosaurs die out?

There are several theories about why dinosaurs died out about 65 million years ago. The main one is that a giant asteroid crashed into Earth around this time. The impact would have created dust, fires, tsunamis (giant waves) and volcanic eruptions that caused a huge change in the planet's climate. It seems likely that the world became freezing cold, and the dinosaurs simply could not survive in the icy conditions.

BELOW *Triceratops* used its horns for defence.

BELOW Scientists think an asteroid may have crashed on Earth, killing some dinosaurs immediately. Others died later as the climate changed.

EARLY BIRDS

How did birds develop?

Scientists believe that birds developed from dinosaurs. They have discovered the fossil remains of feathered dinosaurs that many people believe proves birds are descended from dinosaurs. The fossils were of dromaeosaur dinosaurs. They could not fly but had fluffy down on their bodies and short arms covered with feathers.

DID YOU KNOW?
Hesperornis had webbed feet and small wings for swimming and diving. Its long jaws had many sharp teeth for catching fish and ammonites.

LEFT Fossils show that dromaeosaurs had wrist joints that worked much like those in the wing of a modern bird.

What is the oldest known bird?

Archaeopteryx is the oldest known bird in the world. It flew in ancient skies about 150 million years ago. It was a meat-eating bird about the size of a crow that probably flew fairly short distances at a time. It had feathers like a bird, but it also had teeth and clawed hands rather like a dinosaur.

RIGHT A fossil of an *Archaeopteryx*.

Which was the largest bird?

The largest of the prehistoric birds was *Aepyornis*, also called the elephant bird. It was 3 metres tall and weighed about 450 kilograms. It also laid the biggest eggs of all time – some were almost a metre long. Another flightless bird was *Dinornis*, which grew to 3.5 metres high. It was the tallest bird that ever lived. Both birds had strong, thick legs, a long neck and a bulky body.

BELOW *Aepyornis* looked a bit like a modern ostrich.

What was the monster bird?

The monster bird was *Teratornis*, a prehistoric creature that looked rather like a giant condor. It had a wingspan of roughly 5 to 7 metres. It flew about searching for the dead bodies of other animals to eat. Its remains have been found in tar pits in California, USA, where the bird was presumably trapped when it came down to feed.

RIGHT Like modern vultures, *Teratornis* fed on dead or dying animals.

THE RISE OF MAMMALS

When did mammals develop?

The first mammals developed almost 200 million years ago. During the time of the dinosaurs, mammals were small, furry creatures. They looked rather like the rats and shrews of today, and they ate insects. They scurried around at night and probably lived in holes underground to hide from dinosaurs. After the dinosaurs died out, many new kinds of mammals slowly developed.

BELOW The first mammal was probably *Megazostrodon*, a small rat-like animal.

Did early mammals lay eggs?

Some early mammals laid eggs, unlike most modern mammals, which give birth to live young. Mammals evolved from mammal-like reptiles that grew fur as mammals do but laid eggs like a reptile. Some prehistoric mammals, such as the giant prehistoric kangaroos, were marsupials. Marsupials give birth to very tiny young, which complete their development in a pouch on their mother's body.

RIGHT The modern platypus lays eggs, as early mammals did.

What was the largest meat-eating mammal?

The fierce carnivore *Andrewsarchus* was the largest meat-eating land mammal ever. It was almost 2 metres tall and 5 metres long. *Andrewsarchus* was a dog-like animal with long, powerful jaws. Its teeth were very strong for biting through bone and turtle shell, and it probably searched for food at the edge of rivers.

BELOW *Andrewsarchus* was a dog-like prehistoric mammal.

DID YOU KNOW?

Some scientists believe that the sudden increase in the amount of oxygen on Earth about 50 million years ago explains why bigger mammals, such as huge sabre-toothed cats, evolved.

BELOW *Glyptodon* had an armoured body and grew to 3 metres long.

Do all mammals have teeth?

No, most mammals have teeth, but there is a strange group that have few or no teeth. These are the edentates and include armadillos, sloths and anteaters. One of these was the giant *Glyptodon*, the last of which died 10,000 years ago. *Glyptodon* had no teeth at the front of its mouth, just some strange globe-shaped teeth at the back for grinding plant foods. It could grow to the size of a car.

FROM APES TO HUMANS

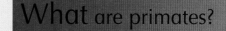
What are primates?

Primates are a group of mammals that includes apes, monkeys and humans. The first primates lived on Earth about 50 million years ago, but they looked rather like squirrels. Over millions of years, different kinds of primates evolved. Between 20 and 10 million years ago, giant apes were common in Africa.

LEFT A giant Asian ape called *Gigantopithecus*.

LEFT Male Neanderthals were heavily built and stood about 1.65 metres tall.

Who were the Neanderthals?

The Neanderthals were an ancient human species that lived in Europe and Asia from about 300,000 to 30,000 years ago, when they became extinct. Long ago, there were other human species, but all of these died out. One was *Homo erectus*, perhaps our earliest human ancestor. *Homo erectus* first appeared almost two million years ago and died out 100,000 years ago.

How did the first people live?

The first people depended on wild plants and animals for food. They used sharp sticks to spear animals or knock them from trees. Their use of tools and their ability to work together were two of the things that made early humans so successful. These early hunters may even have driven some kinds of prehistoric animals to extinction.

BELOW People began to grow their own food and keep animals, such as goats, about 10,000 years ago.

DID YOU KNOW?

Bodies of humans that died as long as 2,300 years ago have been found perfectly preserved in peat bogs. These remains can tell us a great deal about how people lived long ago.

Why did people start farming?

Prehistoric people probably started farming because it was easier than travelling a long way to chase wild animals or gather berries and nuts. As people settled in one place, the first villages and towns developed. Around 5,000 years ago, people began to read and write. This was the end of the prehistoric period because people started to write down their history.

PLANTS AND ANIMALS

There are millions of different kinds of plants and animals living in every place on Earth. They range in size from tiny microscopic plants and animals that are too small to see with the naked eye, to massive whales and giant trees. All of these living things have found ways of surviving in their habitat, whether they live in the blackness of the deep ocean, the heat of the desert or the cold of the mountain tops.

SORTING LIVING THINGS

What is a living thing?

A living thing is said to be living because it can do certain things. It can reproduce, which means it can have young. It can grow and change during its life and use energy from food to live and stay healthy. A living thing can also move in a variety of ways and sense the world around it.

ABOVE These gazelles are living things because they grow, eat, move and reproduce.

BELOW Sunflowers make seeds in the centre of their large flowers. Ferns produce spores on special leaves.

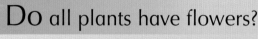

Fern

Do all plants have flowers?

No, but most do! Flowering plants, such as sunflowers and oak trees, reproduce from seeds made in their flowers. Non-flowering plants use different ways to reproduce. For example, pine trees and other conifers make their seeds in cones. Ferns, mosses and seaweeds make tiny grains called spores, usually on their leaves. Spores can only grow into new plants in wet or damp places.

Sunflower

How many different animals are there?

We know of more than a million different kinds of animal on Earth. Scientists make it easier to identify and understand animals by classifying them, or putting them into groups, based on similarities. Animals are classified into two main groups: vertebrates, which have a backbone, and invertebrates, which do not. Vertebrates include humans, snakes and birds. Invertebrates include insects, worms and snails.

DID YOU KNOW?
The seeds of the coco de mer palm tree are the biggest in the world. They can weigh up to 42 kilograms – the same as a large dog.

ABOVE A howler monkey is a vertebrate.

A frog is an amphibian.

Which kinds of vertebrates are which?

Vertebrates are classified into five groups: fish, reptiles, amphibians, birds and mammals. Fish and reptiles both have scaly skin, but fish live in water and reptiles live on land. Amphibians have smooth skin and, although they live on land as adults, their young live in water. Birds have feathers and their young hatch from hard eggs. Mammals have hair and feed their young on milk.

A chimp is a mammal.
An eagle is a bird.

A snake is a reptile.

A cichlid is a fish.

FEEDING AND LIVING

Why do flowers need bees?

Flowering plants need bees and other insects to help them reproduce. Bees visit flowers to feed on their sweet nectar. Pollen collects on a bee's legs when it lands on a flower. When the bee visits another flower, some of this pollen rubs onto the flower. That flower uses the pollen to make seeds that will grow into new plants. Many of the plants and animals that live in the same place need each other to survive.

DID YOU KNOW?
The biggest predator that ever lived was an ancient shark. Scientists looked at the length of its fossilized teeth and worked out that it weighed as much as seven elephants!

How do plants make their food?

Plants make their own food inside their leaves through a process called photosynthesis. The ingredients plants use are water, which is sucked up through the roots, and carbon dioxide, a gas in the air. The leaves absorb sunlight and use this energy to make food from the ingredients. Plants store this sugary food inside them until they need to use it.

Do all animals eat meat?

No, some animals eat only meat, some eat only plants and some eat both plants and meat. Animals, such as sharks and cats, that eat only meat are called carnivores. Most carnivores have sharp teeth or claws to catch animals. Animals, such as cows and caterpillars, that eat only plants are called herbivores. Animals, such as humans, that eat both meat and plants are called omnivores.

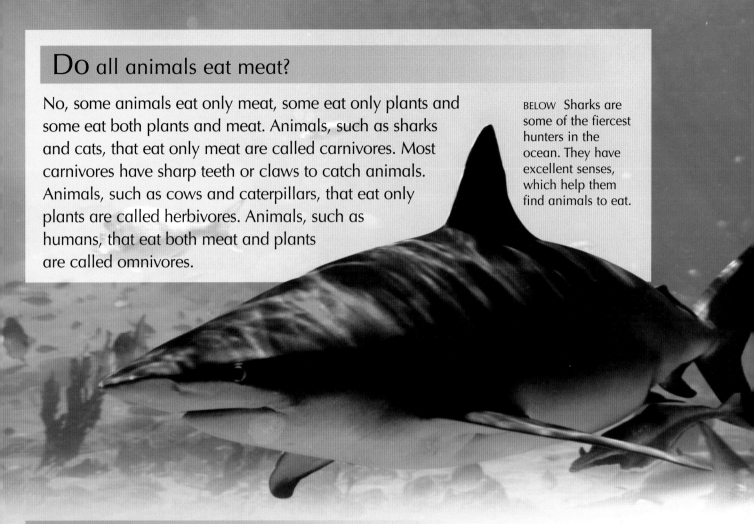

BELOW Sharks are some of the fiercest hunters in the ocean. They have excellent senses, which help them find animals to eat.

What is a food chain?

A food chain is a way of showing what eats what in a particular place. The start of any food chain is a plant, which makes its food by photosynthesis. Next is an animal that eats the plant. Then comes another animal, called a predator, that eats the plant eater. The animal at the end of a food chain is not eaten by any other animal.

BELOW In this food chain, lions feed on zebras, which feed on grass. The arrows in the food chain point to the animal that does the eating.

GRASSLAND HOMES

Why do grassland animals live in herds?

Some animals in the grasslands group together in herds to stay safe. This is because there are few trees and bushes to hide among in the wide open spaces of the grasslands. In a herd, most animals can have their heads down nibbling grass while others keep a lookout for danger. Grassland animals that form herds include elephants, zebras and kangaroos.

How long is a giraffe's neck?

A giraffe's neck is nearly 2.5 metres long, which is longer than many surfboards. Giraffes use their long neck to reach the leaves on tall trees. This is a special feature, or adaptation, that gives giraffes an advantage over grazing animals with shorter necks. This is vital in the grasslands where there are many animals competing to eat the plant foods.

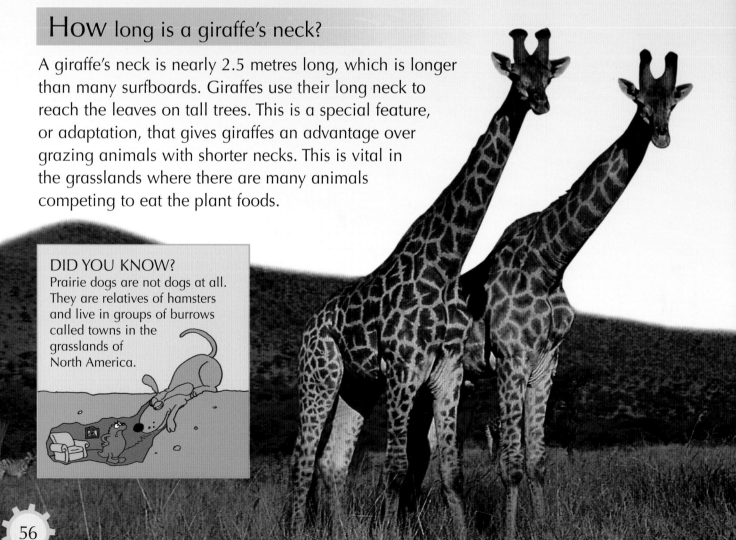

DID YOU KNOW?
Prairie dogs are not dogs at all. They are relatives of hamsters and live in groups of burrows called towns in the grasslands of North America.

Which is the fastest animal on land?

The fastest land animal in the world is the cheetah. It can sprint 100 metres in just over 3 seconds. It uses its speed to catch fast-running prey, such as antelopes. Other grassland predators catch prey in different ways. Lions creep up close to herds of wildebeest and zebra. They work in teams to chase, surround and trap individuals, and then they share their meal.

What is a termite mound?

A termite mound is a nest made by ant-like insects called termites. Termites live in hot grasslands in places such as Africa and Australia. Termite mounds are made from mud that sets hard in the heat. The mounds are up to 7 metres tall and inside there may be millions of termites. Air moving through tubes in the mounds keeps the termites cool.

LEFT A large termite mound in Australia. Not all termites live in mounds. Some live in trees and others live underground.

57

SURVIVING IN A DESERT

Why don't cactus plants have leaves?

Plants lose water through their leaves when it is dry. Cactus plants live in dry deserts, so not having leaves helps them to save water. Instead of leaves, they have thick, green stems, which swell when their roots suck up water after short rain bursts. Cactuses also have spikes to stop animals breaking into their stems to steal the precious water.

Which animal is called a thorny devil?

The thorny devil is a reptile that lives in the desert. It has an armour of spikes along its back to protect it from enemies. The thorny devil has an unusual way of getting the water it needs. When rain or dew lands on its back, the water flows along grooves leading to the corners of its mouth so that it can drink.

LEFT The thorny devil's spikes protect it from predators while it is busy hunting. It eats up to 3,000 ants a day.

How do fennec foxes use their big ears?

Like many desert animals, fennec foxes stay out of the sun because it is too hot. They are nocturnal, meaning they hunt at night and sleep during the day. The foxes use their huge ears to locate prey moving around in the dark, and have thick fur to keep them warm in the cold desert nights.

DID YOU KNOW?
Camels have eyelashes that are more than 10 centimetres long to stop the sand that blows around in desert storms from getting in their eyes.

RIGHT The fennec fox's hearing is sensitive enough to detect beetles, scorpions and spiders scurrying over sand.

What do camels store in their humps?

Camels store fat in their humps to save for times when they cannot find enough food. The fat can be broken down to provide energy. When the fat is used up, the hump becomes droopy until the camel eats again. Camels can survive long periods without water, but after a drought, they can drink enough water in 10 minutes to fill a bath.

59

IN THE RAINFOREST

BELOW Rainforest trees have huge roots to support their tall trunks. The tree-top area is called the canopy.

Why do rainforest trees grow so tall?

Rainforest trees are tall because they grow to reach the sunshine high up in the forest canopy. The warmth and moisture of rainforest regions allows the trees to grow quickly. Rainforest trees, such as teak, can grow to about 50 metres tall – or as high as a lighthouse. Many different fruits and nuts grow on the trees. These are eaten by a great variety of animals.

A flying frog

Can frogs live in trees?

Yes, many different types of frog live in trees in the rainforest. The frogs feed on insects, and some lay eggs in the tiny pools of water that form in the leaves. One rainforest frog, the flying frog, glides across the gaps between the trees. To do this, it stretches out the flaps of skin between its toes like mini parachutes. Another tree frog is the poison arrow frog. It has brightly coloured skin to warn predators that it is very poisonous and should not be eaten.

Do plants ever grow on animals?

Yes, an animal called the sloth looks green because tiny plants called algae grow on its fur. Sloths live in the rainforests in South America, and the green colour helps them to blend in with the green leaves around them. Sloths crawl very slowly among branches using large, hooked claws. They feed on leaves and fruit and only climb to the ground once a week to go to the toilet.

DID YOU KNOW?
Leaf-cutter ants chew off pieces of rainforest leaves and then carry them to their nest. They feed on the fungus that grows on the rotting leaves.

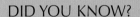

ABOVE Sloths sleep up to 18 hours a day, often hanging from branches. They spend most of their waking hours feeding on leaves.

How do forest-floor animals find food?

Some animals that live on the forest floor, such as agoutis, follow monkeys and parrots to find food. They gather the fruits and nuts that accidentally fall to the ground when the monkeys and parrots are feeding. Agoutis are relatives of guinea pigs and have big, strong front teeth. They use their teeth to gnaw open nuts that many other animals find too hard.

61

MOUNTAIN LIFE

How do mountain plants survive the cold?

Plants survive on cold mountains in various ways. Most are small and grow in cracks among the rocks to keep out of the cold wind. The edelweiss traps warm air among hairs on its leaves and flowers. The alpine snowbell survives under snow during the winter. In spring, the dark colour of its flowers absorbs enough heat from sunlight to melt the snow around it.

ABOVE Edelweiss has yellow flowers surrounded by hairy leaves.

What do giant pandas eat?

Giant pandas eat the stems and leaves of certain kinds of bamboo plant. The bamboo grows in forests on Chinese mountains. Giant pandas mainly eat bamboo, but they also eat insects and eggs that they find in the forest. The pandas feed on bamboo for up to 15 hours a day, eating about 20 kilograms of the plant. Bamboo is a type of grass, which can grow up to 40 metres in height.

Which birds can fly higher than Mount Everest?

Vultures can fly higher than Mount Everest. They can reach heights of up to 11 kilometres, about 2 kilometres higher than the world's highest mountain. Winds blowing up the mountain slopes help the birds to soar up high without having to flap their wings. Vultures are scavengers, meaning they eat animals that are already dead. They have good eyesight so they can spot dead animals on the ground.

DID YOU KNOW?
African mountain gorillas have long, shaggy fur that enables them to stay warm in high mountain forests. The adults cannot climb the trees because they are so heavy they would break the branches.

BELOW Mountain goats have thick, fluffy hair to protect them from the cold.

How do mountain goats get a grip?

Mountain goats can grip the steep, rocky mountain tops because they have special hooves. The hooves have a soft, hollowed pad in the middle that acts a bit like a sucker to grip the bare rocks. Using their hooves, mountain goats can run, jump and climb across the rocks. They go to parts of the mountains where it would be too dangerous for predators, such as snow leopards, to follow.

LIFE IN THE FREEZER

Where do polar bears live?

Polar bears live in the Arctic, the region of the Earth around the icy North Pole. They feed mainly on seals and can hold their breath long enough to hunt seals underwater. Polar bears also catch food by finding the holes in the ice where the seals come to the surface for air. They then jump into the holes to grab their prey.

ABOVE Some people think polar bears eat penguins, but this is impossible because polars bears live at the North Pole and penguins live at the South Pole.

Why do Arctic foxes change colour?

Arctic foxes change colour to camouflage themselves during the year. In winter, they have a white coat to stay hidden against the snow and ice. This helps the foxes to sneak up on prey. In summer, when the snow and ice have melted, the foxes grow a brown coat. Arctic foxes hunt lemmings, which are like voles, as well as birds. They also eat any seal meat left by polar bears.

Do emperor penguins make nests?

No, emperor penguins do not make nests. In Antarctica where they live, there are no twigs or bits of plants to make nests from. Instead, the female lays one egg, which the male carries on top of his feet in a fold of blubbery skin. This keeps the egg warm until it hatches.

DID YOU KNOW?
In winter, people put a liquid called antifreeze in their cars to stop the water in their engines freezing up. Antarctic cod produce their own special kind of antifreeze to stop their blood freezing in icy waters.

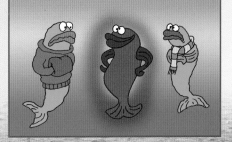

ABOVE The emperor penguin is the largest penguin. The males can be up to 1.2 metres tall.

How do mammals keep warm in icy water?

Mammals that spend a lot of time in icy water keep warm by being very fat. Whales have a thick layer of blubber, or fat, under their skin, which can be up to 30 centimetres thick. Seals and sea lions have fur as well as blubber. This helps to keep them warm when they come onto the land to rest or to have their young.

Whales mainly feed on tiny shrimp-like animals called krill, but they can live on their blubber when food is scarce.

WETLANDS AND LAKES

Which water plant has the biggest leaves?

The Amazon water lily has the biggest leaves. They are up to 2 metres across and very strong. Plants that grow in wetlands and lakes have all the water they need, but they have to find clever ways of getting light for photosynthesis. Plants that grow in deep, dark water, such as water lilies, have floating leaves. Water lily leaves have air spaces inside that help them to float.

Do plants ever eat insects?

Yes, some plants catch insects for food. In bogs and swamps, the soil does not have enough of the substances that plants need to grow. Some carnivorous plants get these healthy substances, or nutrients, by trapping and digesting insects in different ways. The Venus flytrap has special leaves that open and shut like a book. When an insect lands on a Venus flytrap and touches tiny trigger hairs on its leaves, the leaves snap together, trapping the insect inside.

ABOVE The Venus flytrap's leaves are edged with spikes to stop the trapped insects from escaping.

Adult frog

Young frogs hop out of the water.

Tadpoles grow legs.

Eggs

Tadpoles

When do tadpoles become frogs?

Tadpoles become frogs when they are fully grown and it is time to live on land. Tadpoles hatch from eggs that frogs lay in the water. They have a long tail to swim with and look like fishes. As the tadpoles turn into frogs, they increase in size and grow legs. Once they are frogs, they live on land, but they return to the water to lay their eggs.

Why do beavers build dams?

Beavers build dams across rivers to make deep ponds. They then build their homes, or lodges, in the ponds. The dams and lodges are made of logs, mud and rocks. The top of the lodge is above the water, but the entrance is deep underwater. This stops predators, such as bears and wolves, from getting in. Inside, the lodge is warm and dry, and young beavers can live there in safety.

BELOW Beavers have thick fur to help keep them warm in cold water. They use their sharp teeth to cut the logs they need to build their dams and lodges.

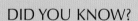

DID YOU KNOW?
Wetlands are popular stopover places for migrating ducks and geese because there is lots of water and food to eat.

COASTS AND CORAL REEFS

Does seaweed have roots?

Seaweed does not have roots because it does not need them. It gets its food from the water around it and not from soil like other plants. It uses parts called holdfasts to grip onto rocks to stop the tides and waves washing it away. Many crabs and other invertebrates, such as limpets and starfish, feed on seaweed.

ABOVE Seaweed mainly grows near coasts. It can be green, red or brown.

Is coral dead or alive?

Coral is alive, but coral reefs are not. Coral polyps are tiny marine creatures that live in warm seas. To protect themselves from predators, they produce stony skeletons. Over many years, the skeletons of millions of dead coral polyps slowly build up to form coral reefs. These reefs are important habitats for many kinds of fish.

Why do crabs walk sideways?

Crabs walk sideways because their legs bend that way. Crabs have 10 legs, but they use only eight of them to move. The other two are claws. They use the claws to grasp food, fight other crabs and to nip predators that get too close. A crab's flat shape and folding legs let it squeeze into holes to keep out of the way of predators.

DID YOU KNOW?
Sea otters catch seafood, such as clams, store them in their armpits and then float on their back while they dine.

When do sea turtles come ashore?

Sea turtles come ashore to lay their eggs on dry land. Turtles spend their life at sea but, once a year, the females crawl up sandy beaches at night. They use their back flippers to dig holes, where they lay more than 100 eggs. The females bury the eggs and then swim away. When the baby turtles hatch, they make their way to the water.

69

OCEAN LIFE

BELOW The bottle-nosed dolphin's curved mouth makes it look like it is smiling.

How do dolphins hunt?

Dolphins hunt for fish in deep or dirty water using 'echolocation'. This means they make clicking noises and can tell where their prey is located by how the clicks echo, or bounce back. In clear waters, dolphins often hunt together in teams. They circle their prey and even chase it into shallow water to catch it.

Why does an octopus change colour?

An octopus changes its colour for camouflage. It alters the colour of its skin by squeezing tiny bags of ink under its skin. The octopus does this so it can blend in with the rock or sand nearby. Using this disguise, it can lie in wait to catch prey animals, such as lobsters, as they pass by.

What is an angler fish?

An angler fish is a type of fish that lives in the dark waters about a kilometre below the ocean's surface. There, the only light comes from animals that make their own light. The angler fish has a glowing lure, like a fishing rod, dangling in front of its mouth. Any small fish that is attracted to the lure is grabbed in the angler fish's mouth.

LEFT The angler fish can open its mouth wide enough to swallow prey that is twice its size.

Can great white sharks smell blood?

Yes, great white sharks can smell blood from a long way away. This helps them find prey many kilometres away. Great white sharks mostly eat fur seals and sea lions. They can detect the blood in the water when seals and sea lions are giving birth. The sharks swim beneath their prey and catch them with their razor-sharp teeth.

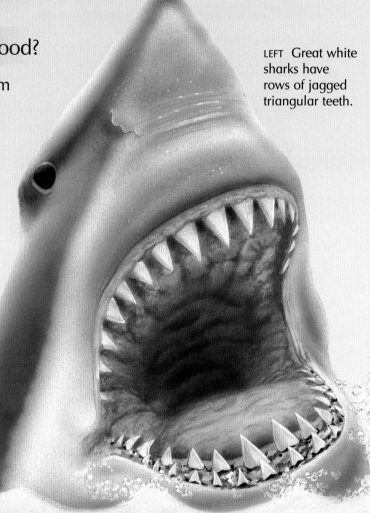

LEFT Great white sharks have rows of jagged triangular teeth.

DID YOU KNOW?
The fangtooth is a vicious-looking deep-sea fish that has the largest teeth for its size in the ocean. Its teeth are so big, it cannot close its mouth properly!

SCIENCE AND TECHNOLOGY

The world around us behaves according to scientific laws. Scientists have discovered many of these laws, and are making new discoveries all the time. We develop technology using our understanding of science and the forces, such as magnetism, gravity and electricity, which shape our lives. Whenever you turn on a light, log on to the Internet or speak to your friends on a mobile phone, it has all been made possible by science.

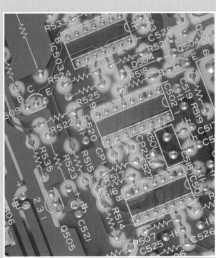

THE WORLD AROUND US

What are things made of?

Everything, from water or air to a whale or a mobile phone, is made of tiny particles called atoms. There are over 100 different kinds of atoms, which are in turn made of smaller parts called subatomic particles. Two or more atoms join together to make a molecule. The things around us are solids, liquids or gases depending on the arrangement of the atoms and molecules inside them.

LEFT Buildings need to be made from hard solids, such as stone.

BELOW An atom is made of subatomic particles. Particles called electrons circle around the centre, called the nucleus.

nucleus

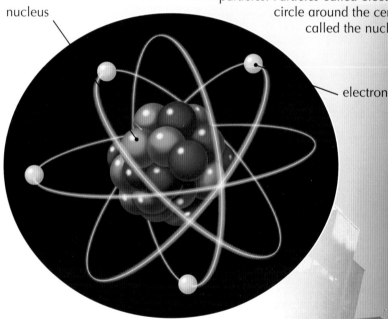

electron

Why are stones hard?

Stones are hard because they are solids. Atoms or molecules in solids are packed tightly and neatly together. This means solids hold their shape. Some solids are bendy or squashy, such as rubber or feathers. The hardness of a solid depends on how tightly its atoms are held together.

Why is honey runny?

Honey is runny because it is a liquid. The molecules inside a liquid are less tightly packed than they are in a solid, and are not rigidly linked. That is why liquids can flow and take the shape of the container we pour them into. Some liquids are thick, such as honey. Others are thin, such as water.

DID YOU KNOW?
Atoms are so tiny that, even if you put 4 million atoms side-by-side, they would be only the width of a pinhead!

How do balloons float?

Helium balloons float because the gas inside them is lighter than air. In all gases, molecules move around quickly in all directions. Gases do not stay in one shape as solids do. They can spread out to fill any shape or space. In a hot air balloon, the air molecules spread out as they heat up. As there are fewer molecules in each bit of space, the balloon floats.

LEFT Hot air balloons float because the hot air inside them is lighter than the cold air around them.

75

FORCES AND MOVEMENT

When do things move?

Things move only when a force is applied to them. Forces are pushes or pulls in a particular direction. A flag blows when the wind pushes it. A door opens when you pull it. Animals move when their feet push against the ground, their wings push against the air or their fins push against the water around them.

How do forces work?

Forces work in pairs. They push or pull in opposite directions. When pairs of forces are equal they are said to be balanced. Tug-of-war teams remain still when each pulls with the same strength. A team falls when one side is stronger and the forces are unbalanced. Forces are also balanced when things move at one speed in the same direction.

BELOW A rocket takes off when the force from the engine pushing it up is greater than the force of gravity pulling it down.

Why do things stop moving?

Things slow down and stop because of an opposing force. One of these forces is friction. Friction happens when tiny bumps on two surfaces rub against each other. Rough surfaces, such as concrete, create more friction than smooth surfaces, such as glass. People use high-friction materials like rubber on shoe soles to stop people slipping when they walk.

DID YOU KNOW?
Very fast cars, such as dragsters and rocket cars, need parachutes to slow them down quickly.

LEFT A bicycle's brakes use high-friction rubber to slow the wheels down.

How do parachutes work?

A parachute slows down a person's fall using 'air resistance'. Air resistance happens when air molecules in front of a moving object squash together and press back against it. The wide area of an open parachute creates lots more resistance than a person could create with his or her body alone. This reduces the falling speed of the body.

LEFT The wide parachute creates enough air resistance to slow the body's fall.

LIGHT AND DARK

Where does light come from?

The Earth's biggest source of light is the Sun. Heat and light energy created by the Sun travels through space in straight lines called rays at almost 300,000 kilometres per second. The Earth spins right round once a day, changing which parts of the globe get sunlight. This creates day and night. Other things that radiate, or give off, light include electric lightbulbs, candles and television sets.

ABOVE We make our own light in cities when the Sun goes down at night.

What are shadows?

Shadows happen in places where an object stops light from getting through. Materials that light shines through fully are said to be transparent. Translucent materials let only a little light through. Opaque materials do not let any light through at all. The shape of a shadow depends on the shape of the object blocking the light. If an object is moved closer to a light source, its shadow gets bigger because it blocks more light rays.

Why do mirrors reflect images?

All surfaces reflect light but, if they are bumpy, the light rays are reflected in all directions. Mirrors are made from very smooth surfaces that reflect the rays back in the same pattern as they hit it, creating a clear image of any object. Words reflected in a mirror appear back to front, as if they were facing away from us and we were looking through the page.

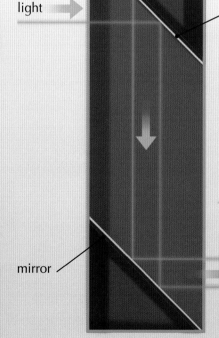

light

mirror

mirror

ABOVE Periscopes use mirrors to allow people to see things above them.

DID YOU KNOW?
Fireflies flash chemicals that give off light in their bodies to attract mates at night.

How do periscopes work?

Periscopes are devices that use reflecting mirrors in order to see things from a lower level. An angled mirror reflects an image, made up of light, down a tube. A second angled mirror at the bottom of the tube reflects the light again to turn the image back the right way up. Periscopes are often used to see surface ships from underwater submarines or over people's heads in crowds.

COLOURS

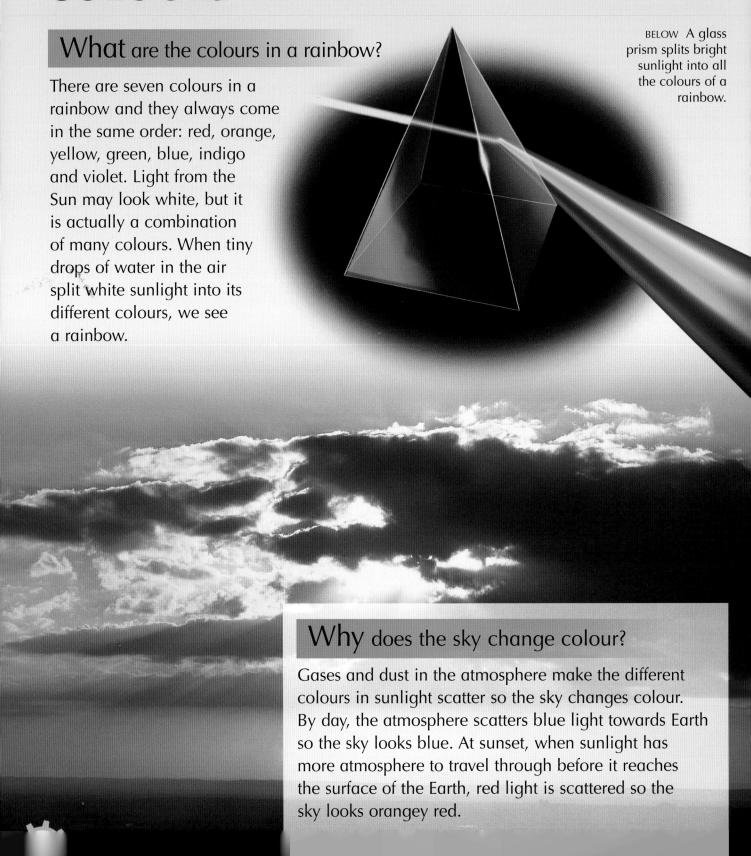

What are the colours in a rainbow?

There are seven colours in a rainbow and they always come in the same order: red, orange, yellow, green, blue, indigo and violet. Light from the Sun may look white, but it is actually a combination of many colours. When tiny drops of water in the air split white sunlight into its different colours, we see a rainbow.

BELOW A glass prism splits bright sunlight into all the colours of a rainbow.

Why does the sky change colour?

Gases and dust in the atmosphere make the different colours in sunlight scatter so the sky changes colour. By day, the atmosphere scatters blue light towards Earth so the sky looks blue. At sunset, when sunlight has more atmosphere to travel through before it reaches the surface of the Earth, red light is scattered so the sky looks orangey red.

Which colours do we print with?

People print colour images and words on paper using just four coloured inks: yellow, cyan (blue), magenta (red) and black. Paper is printed with tiny dots of different amounts of each ink. Our brain cannot distinguish the dots we see separately, but instead, blends them together to make different blocks of different colours.

LEFT You can get new colours by mixing other colours together. For instance, mixing blue and yellow makes green.

How do animals use colour?

Some animals have similar coloured skin or fur to their habitats so they cannot be seen easily. This is called camouflage. Polar bears are white so they can sneak up on seals to catch them, but caterpillars are green to hide on leaves. Other animals use colours so they can easily be seen and avoided. For example, arrow frogs are brightly coloured to warn that they are poisonous.

DID YOU KNOW?
Chameleons change colour as their mood varies because blobs of pigment (colouring) under their skin get bigger or smaller.

RIGHT Wasps are brightly coloured to warn other animals that they have a nasty sting.

SOUND

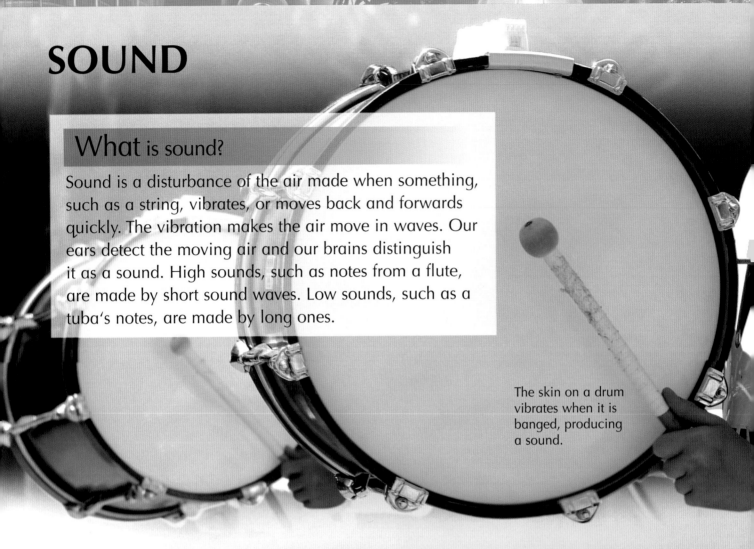

What is sound?

Sound is a disturbance of the air made when something, such as a string, vibrates, or moves back and forwards quickly. The vibration makes the air move in waves. Our ears detect the moving air and our brains distinguish it as a sound. High sounds, such as notes from a flute, are made by short sound waves. Low sounds, such as a tuba's notes, are made by long ones.

The skin on a drum vibrates when it is banged, producing a sound.

When do sounds get quieter?

Sound vibrations travel away from the thing that makes them. The vibrations spread out in all directions like the ripples in a pond after you throw in a pebble. The wider the vibrations spread, the smaller they become and the quieter the sound. Big vibrations, on the other hand, make lots of energy that pushes lots of air, creating loud sounds.

How do we measure sounds?

Sound is measured in units called decibels. The quietest sounds, such as a leaf falling, are around 0–10 decibels. The loudest sounds, such as a rocket launch, are just less than 200 decibels. Noises above 90 decibels are dangerous to listen to because the strong waves of air can damage the sensitive insides of your ears.

DID YOU KNOW?
It is silent in space because there is no air to convert vibrations into sound waves.

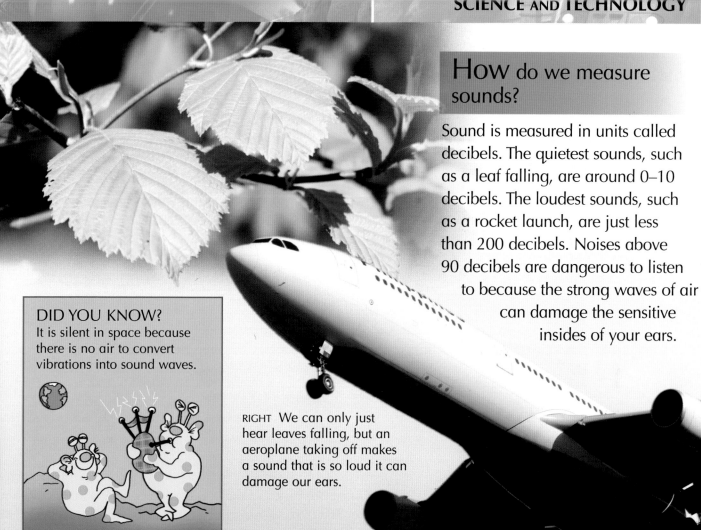

RIGHT We can only just hear leaves falling, but an aeroplane taking off makes a sound that is so loud it can damage our ears.

What are echoes?

Echoes are the repeated noise we hear when sound waves bounce off solid objects, such as a cliff or the inside of a tunnel. If the object is close by, the waves reflect so quickly we cannot hear the echo as a separate sound. Bats use echoes to get around in the dark. They make squeaks and listen to the echoes to work out how far away things are and how big they are.

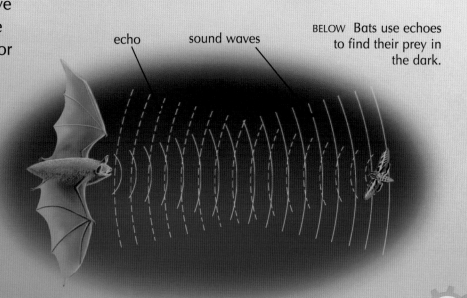

echo   sound waves   BELOW Bats use echoes to find their prey in the dark.

FUELS OF THE EARTH

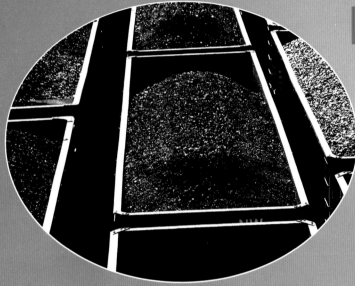

What are fossil fuels?

Fossil fuels are oil, natural gas and coal, which formed from the fossilized remains of plants and animals. In prehistoric times, dead animals and plants became buried inside sedimentary rocks and slowly turned into fossils. Over millions of years, heat and pressure changed the fossils into fuel in the form of oil, gas and coal, which can be burned to release heat.

ABOVE Coal formed from trees that grew in swamps in prehistoric times.

BELOW Oil rigs are platforms in the sea where people drill into the seabed to find oil.

Where do oil and gas come from?

Oil and gas come from rocks deep within the ground. People use very long drills and pipes to release the oil and gas. The rocks are sometimes under land but are often found under the ocean. People drill holes deep into the sea floor and squirt chemicals down the holes to release the fuels. The oil and gas can be made into petrol, plastic and other products.

NORTH CORMORANT

When will fossil fuels run out?

The world's oil and gas will run out by 2050, and coal by 2100, if we continue using them at the same rate as today and do not discover any new stores of them in the ground. Fossil fuels are non-renewable, which means that once they are used up they are gone. To save energy, people must use more renewable energy, such as sunlight, wind or moving water, that will never run out.

DID YOU KNOW?
The biggest oil tanker is longer than the Eiffel Tower is tall and can carry enough oil to fill over 300 Olympic-sized swimming pools!

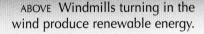
ABOVE Windmills turning in the wind produce renewable energy.

Can people turn waste into fuel?

Yes, heat energy is released when plant waste, such as unwanted wood or crops, is burned. 'Biodegradable waste', such as leftover food, animal manure, scrap paper and weeds, is broken down, or degraded, by bacteria to make biogas and biofuel. Some crops, such as sugar cane and corn, are specially grown to make biofuel.

ABOVE Pig manure can be made into biofuel.

ELECTRICITY

What is electricity?

Electricity is a type of energy formed from tiny particles inside atoms called electrons. These electrons can move from one atom to another and this movement is electrical energy. Electricity powers many machines, from torches and mobile phones to televisions and computers. It moves, or flows, into machines through materials called conductors, which include metal wires.

LEFT Lightning, the streaks or flashes of light that can be seen during a thunderstorm, are sparks of electricity.

Where does electricity come from?

BELOW Some electricity comes from hydroelectric power stations, where moving water turns the turbines.

Mains electricity is produced in power stations by machines called generators. Fuel, such as coal, is burned in the power station to turn water into steam. The steam turns a turbine (a set of large circular blades), which rotates magnets inside the generator, producing electricity. The electricity flows through wires to sockets in our homes.

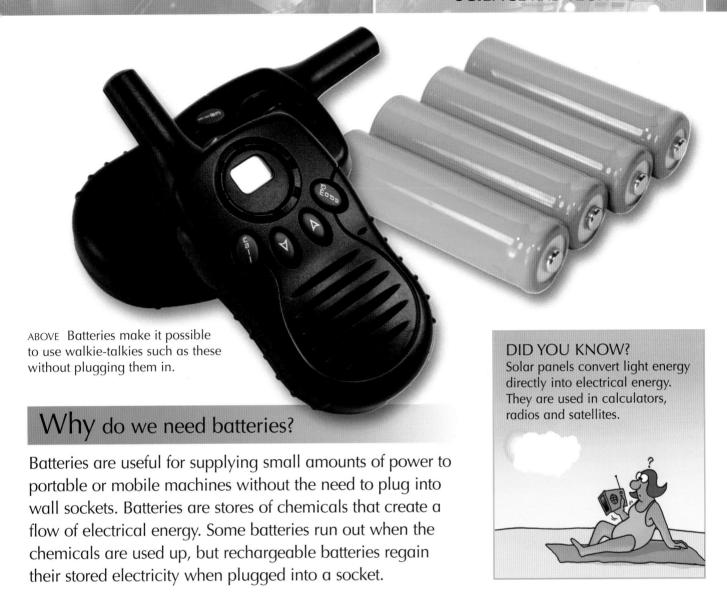

ABOVE Batteries make it possible to use walkie-talkies such as these without plugging them in.

Why do we need batteries?

Batteries are useful for supplying small amounts of power to portable or mobile machines without the need to plug into wall sockets. Batteries are stores of chemicals that create a flow of electrical energy. Some batteries run out when the chemicals are used up, but rechargeable batteries regain their stored electricity when plugged into a socket.

DID YOU KNOW?
Solar panels convert light energy directly into electrical energy. They are used in calculators, radios and satellites.

How do switches work?

Switches work by controlling the flow, or current, of electricity through machines. Electricity can only flow through a circuit, which is a continuous loop of wire. A switch is rather like a gate that can open or close to break or complete the circuit.

battery

switch

light bulb

circuit

LEFT A switch turns a light on and off by breaking or completing the flow of electricity through the circuit.

87

MAKING MACHINES WORK

Which machines have motors?

Many machines have electric motors. A motor contains a coil (tightly looped wire) on a shaft in the centre of some magnets. When an electric current passes through the coil, the coil becomes magnetized and is repelled by the magnet. This makes the coil rotate and turn the shaft. The turning movement can be used to power machines.

electric toy train

drill

ABOVE Many power tools, such as this one used to cut through metal, are driven by motors. Drills and toy trains also contain motors.

metal filament

RIGHT In an ordinary lightbulb, resistor wires, called the filament, glow to produce light.

Why do lightbulbs glow?

Some lightbulbs glow because a thin metal wire, or filament, inside them converts electrical energy into light energy. Other lightbulbs do not use wires, but make light in a different way. Energy-saving lightbulbs have a special fluorescent coating inside gas-filled glass tubes. When a current passes through the gas, it makes the coating glow.

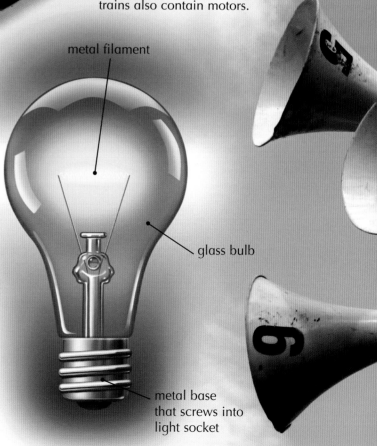

glass bulb

metal base that screws into light socket

What makes toasters hot?

Toasters get hot because finely coiled wires make heat to toast bread. These finely coiled wires are called resistors. They slow down the flow of electricity. As the movement of electrons is slowed, some of the electrical energy changes into heat energy. Hairdryers work in a similar way. A fan blows air past hot wires to warm up the air.

LEFT These big loudspeakers are used to make public announcements. Smaller ones are found in radios, televisions and CD players.

How do loudspeakers work?

Loudspeakers work by turning electricity into sound. A thin cone of cardboard or plastic, called a diaphragm, vibrates when electrical signals are sent through a wire coil. The loudness and pitch (high or low notes) of the sound produced depend on the size and speed of the vibrations.

89

DIGITAL TECHNOLOGY

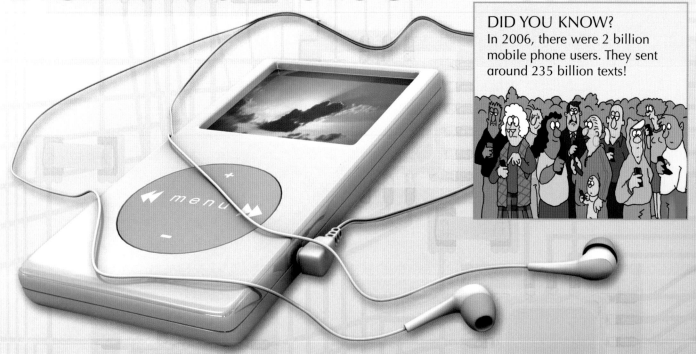

What is digital technology?

Digital technology includes computers, digital cameras, MP3 players and mobiles. These record, store, send and process electronic signals as digital information. 'Digital' means that the electrical signals are either 'on' ('1') or 'off' ('0'). The 1s and 0s form a code that can represent any type of information.

BELOW Many microchips are less than a centimetre square.

How do microchips work?

Microchips work using tiny electrical circuits. The circuits are built on paper-thin chips of silicon, a material that is very good at conducting electricity (allowing electricity to pass through it). A single microchip can contain thousands of circuits, allowing it to process lots of digital information. Microchips mean that computers and other digital devices can be small and light.

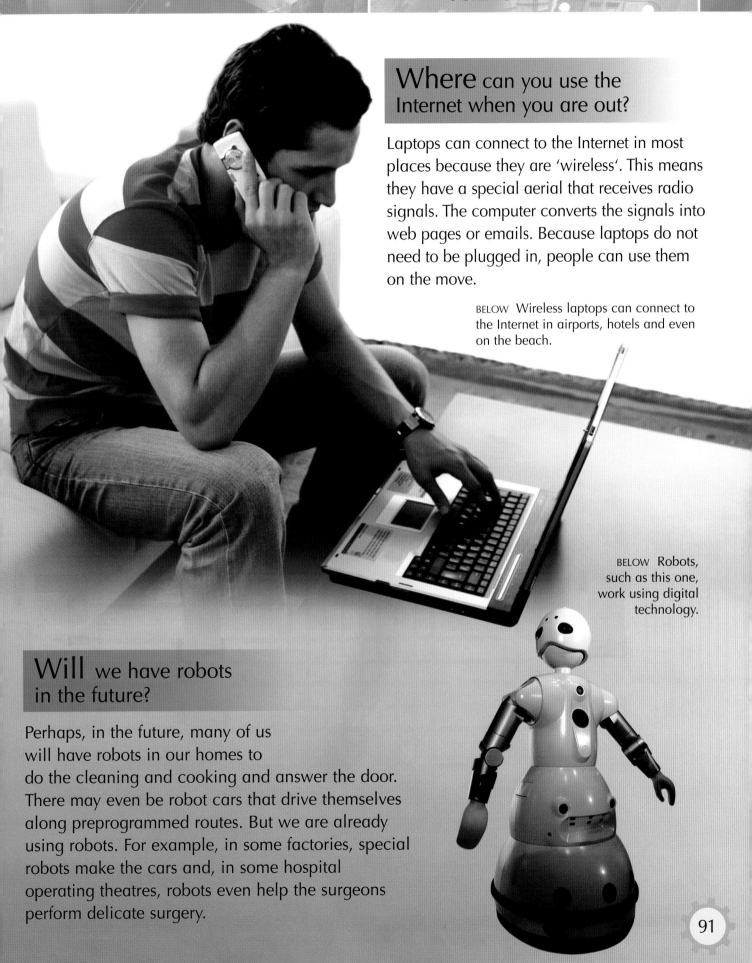

Where can you use the Internet when you are out?

Laptops can connect to the Internet in most places because they are 'wireless'. This means they have a special aerial that receives radio signals. The computer converts the signals into web pages or emails. Because laptops do not need to be plugged in, people can use them on the move.

BELOW Wireless laptops can connect to the Internet in airports, hotels and even on the beach.

BELOW Robots, such as this one, work using digital technology.

Will we have robots in the future?

Perhaps, in the future, many of us will have robots in our homes to do the cleaning and cooking and answer the door. There may even be robot cars that drive themselves along preprogrammed routes. But we are already using robots. For example, in some factories, special robots make the cars and, in some hospital operating theatres, robots even help the surgeons perform delicate surgery.

INDEX

ACKNOWLEDGEMENTS

Artwork supplied through the Art Agency by Terry Pastor, Ken Oliver, Peter Ball, Myke Taylor, Stuart Jackson-Carter, Wayne Ford

Photo credits:
b = bottom, t = top, r = right, l = left, m = middle

Front cover: Andy Rouse/Corbis, Darrell Gulin/Corbis, tl (inset) Dreamstime.com, tm (inset) Dreamstime.com/Antonio Petrone, tr (inset) Toshiyuki Aizawa/Reuters/Corbis
Back cover: 42t Dreamstime.com/Mark Bond
Front flap: NASA
Back flap: Dreamstime.com/Ismael Montero

1 Dreamstime.com/Ismael Montero, 2 NASA, 3l NASA, 3m Dreamstime.com/Thomas Scheiker, 3r Dreamstime.com, 4 Dreamstime.com/Elenthewise, 10t NASA, 10b Joseph Sohm; ChromoSohm Inc./CORBIS, 11t Dreasmtime.com/Ken Wood, 12B Dreamstime.com/Goce Risteski, 12-13r NASA, 12tm Digital Vision, 13t NASA, 13b NASA, 14t NASA, 14b NASA, 15t Dreamstime.com/Antonio Petrone, 15b NASA, 16t NASA, 16b NASA, 17t NASA, 17m NASA, 17b NASA, 18-19b NASA, 20t Dreamstime.com/Steven Bourelle, 20b Dreamstime.com/Daniel Gustavsson, 22b NASA, 22-23m Digital Vision, 23t iStockphoto.com, 23b iStockphoto.com, 24b Dreamstime.com/Jose Fuente, 25t Digial Vision, 25b NASA, 26b Digital Vision, 27b NASA, 28 Dreamstime.com, 29bl Dreamstime.com/Anthony J. Hall, 29bm Dreamstime.com/Natalia Bratslavsky, 29br Dreamstime.com/Bob Ainsworth, 30t Dreamstime.com/Ismael Montero, 31t Dreamstime.com/Bob Aimsworth, 31b Dreamstime.com/Tanya Weliky, 32t Dreamstime.com/Natalia Bratslavsky, 33t Dreamstime.com/Asther Lau Choon Siew, 34tl Wolfgang Kaehler/CORBIS, 34tr Layne Kennedy/CORBIS, 35t Dreamstime.com/Dannyphoto80, 36b Dreamstime.com, 44bDreamstime.com/Bob Ainsworth, 52t Corbis, 52bl Dreamstime.com/Stasys Eidiejus, 68br Dreamstime.com, 53tr Dreamstime.com/Christopher Marin, 53br Dreamstime.com/Stephen McSweeny, 53bmt Dreamstime.com/Andre Nantel, 53bml Dreamstime.com/Tim Goodwin, 53bmr Dreamstime.com/Stephen Inglis, 53bmb Dreamstime.com/Dallas Powell Jr, 54t Dreamstime.com/Thomas Scheiker, 54b Dreamstime.com/Jens Mayer, 55t Dreamstime.com/Ian Scott, 55bl Dreamstime.com/Anna Kowalska, 55bm Dreamstime.com/Joe Stone, 55br Digital Vision, 56t Digital Vision, 56b Digital Vision, 57t Dreamstime.com/Craig Ruaux, 57b Dreamstime.com/Craig Ruaux, 58t Dreamstime.com, 59t Dreamstime.com/Nathan 430, 59b Dreamstime.com/Pomortzeff, 60t Dreamstime.com/Hhakim, 61t Dreamstime.com/Pantoja, 61b Dreamstime.com/Ryszard, 62t Dreamstime.com/Avner Richard, 62b Dreamstime.com/F2, 63t Dreamstime.com/Carlos Arranz, 63b Corbis, 64t Corbis, 64b Dreamstime.com/Dcrippen, 65t Dreamstime.com/Bernardbreton, 65b Corbis, 66t Dreamstime.com/Alantduffy1970, 66b Dreamstime.com/Janehb, 67b Corbis, 68t Dreamstime.com/Dpw-shane, 68b Dreamstime.com/Matthias Weinrich, 69t Dreamstime.com, 69b Dreamstime.com, 70t Corbis, 70b Dreamstime.com/John Abramo, 72 Dreamstime.com/Rafa Irusta, 73bl Digital Vision, 73bm Digital Vision, 73br Dreamstime.com, 74r Dreamstime.com/Marcelo Zagal, 74ml Dreamstime.com/Andreus, 75tl Dreamstime.com/Kasia75, 75b Dreamstime.com, 76t Dreamstime.com, 76b NASA, 77t Dreamstime.com/Bigmax, 78t Dreamstime.com/Holger Feroudj, 78b Dreamstime.com, 79t Dreamstiem.com/Roy Mattappallil, 80b Digital Vision, 81b Dreamstime.com, 82t Dreamstime.com/Dkye, 82b Dreamstime.com/Jason Stitt, 83t Dreamstime.com/Alan Snelling, 83b Dreamstime.com/Terdonal, 84t Dreamstime.com, 84b Dreamstime.com/Lancemichaels, 85t Dreamstime.com/Rafa Irusta, 85b Dreamstime.com, 86t Dreamstime.com/Jerry Horn, 86b Dreamstime.com/John Sartin, 87tl Dreamstime.com, 87tr Dreamstime.com/Scott Rothstein, 88tr Dreamstime.com/Attila Huszti, 88tm Dreamstime.com/Adam Borkowski, 88tl Dreamstime.com/Jose Antonio, 89tr Dreamstime.com/Visualfield, 89b Dreamstime.com, 90t Dreamstime.com/Crni_arapin, 90b Dreamstime.com, 91t Dreamstime.com, 91b Toshiyuki Aizawa/Reuters/Corbis